HOW NATURE WORKS

ANIMALS

WEB LINKED

First published in 2011 by Miles Kelly Publishing Ltd
Harding's Barn, Bardfield End Green, Thaxted, Essex, CM6 3PX, UK

Copyright © Miles Kelly Publishing Ltd 2011

10 9 8 7 6 5 4 3 2 1

Publishing Director: Belinda Gallagher
Creative Director: Jo Cowan
Design Concept: Simon Lee
Volume Design: Rocket Design
Cover Designers: Kayleigh Allen, Simon Lee
Indexer: Gill Lee
Production Manager: Elizabeth Collins
Reprographics: Stephan Davis, Jennifer Hunt,
Anthony Cambray
Consultant: Camilla de la Bedoyere

ISBN 978-1-84810-468-6

Printed in China

British Library Cataloguing-in-Publication Data
A catalogue record for this book is available from the British Library

Every effort has been made to acknowledge the source and copyright holder of each picture. Miles Kelly Publishing apologises for any unintentional errors or omissions.

MADE WITH PAPER FROM

A SUSTAINABLE FOREST

HOW NATURE WORKS

ANIMALS

By Steve Parker

Illustrated by Julian Baker

Miles Kelly

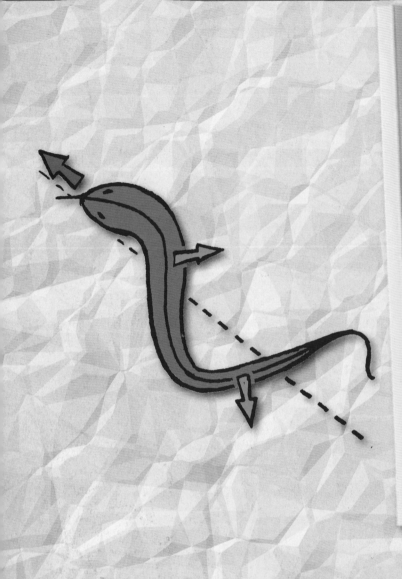

ACKNOWLEDGEMENTS

All panel artworks by Rocket Design

The publishers would like to thank the following sources for the use of their photographs:

Front cover: Dreamstime: (c) Vaklav; Photolibrary.com: (tl) L Peck Michael

Back cover: Dreamstime: (tr) Naluphoto

Alamy: 26 Jack Milchanowski; 28(c) David J Slater; 30 blickwinkel

Corbis: 32 David A. Northcott; 34(c) Gary Meszaros

Dreamstime: 10(b) Nastya22; 14(b) Monkeystock; 16(c) Naluphoto; 22(b) Deepdesert; 24 Vaklav; 31(b) Katclay

FLPA: 14(c) Cyril Ruoso/Minden Pictures; 18(b) Colin Marshall; 37(b) Norbert Wu/Minden Pictures

Getty Images: 6(bl) Frank Lukasseck

NHPA: 7(c) Oceans Image/Photoshot

naturepl.com: 12(c) Brandon Cole; 20(c) David Fleetham

Photolibrary.com: 8(c) L Peck Michael; 18(c) Clive Bromhall

Shutterstock: 7(tr) JonMilnes; 8(b) John Carnemolla; 10(c) FloridaStock; 12(l) Gergo Orban; 20(b) iDesign; 22(c) Thomas Barrat; 27(r) Tyler Fox; 28(l) Dr. Morley Read; 33(b) Eugene Sim; 36 B.G. Smith

Science Photo Library: 34(b) Andrew J. Martinez

Topfoto.co.uk: 6(t) Artmedia/HIP/TopFoto

All other photographs are from Miles Kelly Archives

WWW.FACTSFORPROJECTS.COM

Each top right-hand page directs you to the Internet to help you find out more. You can log on to **www.factsforprojects.com** to find free pictures, additional information, videos, fun activities and further web links. These are for your own personal use and should not be copied or distributed for any commercial or profit-related purpose.

If you do decide to use the Internet with your book, here's a list of what you'll need:
• A PC with Microsoft® Windows® XP or later versions, or a Macintosh with OS X or later, and 512Mb RAM

• A browser such as Microsoft® Internet Explorer 9, Firefox 4.X or Safari 5.X
• Connection to the Internet. Broadband connection recommended
• An account with an Internet Service Provider (ISP)
• A sound card for listening to sound files

Links won't work?
www.factsforprojects.com is regularly checked to make sure the links provide you with lots of information. Sometimes you may receive a message saying that a site is unavailable. If this happens, just try again later.

Stay safe!
When using the Internet, make sure you follow these guidelines:
• Ask a parent's or a guardian's permission before you log on.
• Never give out your personal details, such as your name, address or email.
• If a site asks you to log in or register by typing your name or email address, speak to your parent or guardian first.
• If you do receive an email from someone you don't know, tell an adult and do not reply to the message.
• Never arrange to meet anyone you have talked to on the Internet.

Miles Kelly Publishing is not responsible for the accuracy or suitability of the information on any website other than its own. We recommend that children are supervised while on the Internet and that they do not use Internet chat rooms.

www.mileskelly.net

info@mileskelly.net

CONTENTS

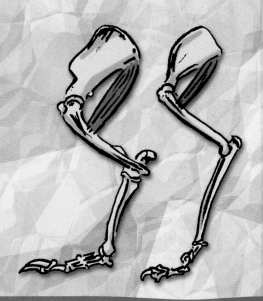

INTRODUCTION

From the biggest blue whales, elephants, polar bears and gorillas to the tiniest worms and spiders, all animals must grow, feed, breed, and generally survive in order to carry on their kind. There are at least two million known types, or species, of creatures on Earth, and they are adapted for life in habitats all around the world, from icy seas to tropical forests. Animals have developed many different solutions to life's great challenges.

Early explorers brought back tales of fanciful beasts – without studying the animals up close they imagined strange and unusual creatures.

NEW LIFE

Reproduction is one of the key features of all living things. Most animals tend to produce more offspring than can survive in their habitat. The idea is that the offspring differ in small ways, such as running speed or ability to smell. Those young with the slight variations that help their survival grow up, breed and pass these successful variations to their own offspring. The young that are less suited to the habitat do not survive. This is the process of natural selection, as animals evolve and become better adapted to their surroundings at the time.

Yolk is a store of nutrients

Air space

Developing embryo

A hard shell protects a baby bird as it develops inside the egg.

A female Virginia opossum has many young, yet only one or two will survive to adulthood

The female ocean sunfish produces more than 300 million eggs each year. Some female albatrosses lay only one egg every two years.

The topics featured in this book are Internet linked.
Visit www.factsforprojects.com to find out more.

THE NEED TO FEED

Plants feed themselves using energy from the Sun and nutrients from soil. Animals cannot make their own food, so they ultimately rely on plants as an energy source. Herbivorous animals get fuel for their bodies by eating plants, while carnivores indirectly gain energy from plants by feeding on plant-eating animals. Omnivores eat either plants or meat – or both. We eat food using our mouths and teeth, but some animals have very strange methods of eating, such as filtering tiny edible bits from mud on the sea floor.

Feather duster or Christmas tree worms filter sea water for nourishment.

Sharks are the ultimate marine carnivores, seeking other creatures to eat.

The polar bear faces some of the coldest temperatures on Earth. But its amazing insulation protects even at –40°C, even outdoing human houses.

Cavity wall and loft insulation keep house warm

Boiler and radiators produce heat

Blubber and fur work as insulation

Thermostat controls temperature

Liver, heart and other inner organs produce heat

Brain acts as a thermostat

KEEPING COSY

Cold conditions slow down life processes inside the body. Some animals cope by becoming inactive in a state known as 'torpor'. Cold-blooded animals such as snakes, frogs and insects enter this state during winter. Warm-blooded or endothermic ('heat from within') creatures – chiefly mammals and birds – can keep going even in the coldest conditions. They rely on fur or feathers, body fat (blubber) and other adaptations to maintain their internal temperature.

RUNNING AT SPEED

The animal kingdom's fastest four-legged mover is the cheetah – but usually for less than a minute. This cat is solely a sprinter and cannot stay in top gear for long. Like all animals, its movements are powered by body parts called muscles. The shoulder and hip muscles pull on the cheetah's leg bones, swinging them to and fro at the rate of almost three massive bounding strides every second.

Did you know?

A cheetah's top speed is limited by three things: Its lungs, which cannot breathe fast and deep enough to get sufficient air; its heart, which is unable to supply enough blood to the muscles; and its muscles, which heat up so quickly the cat must pause and pant to prevent heatstroke.

Cheetahs mainly hunt fast-moving antelopes, gazelles and hares. Other common prey are much slower, such as warthogs, ground squirrels and lizards.

Flexible spine

Back The long, bendy backbone arches up with legs together (as here) then curves down with legs extended, to pivot the shoulders and hips for even greater strides.

Tail The tail streams out straight behind for least air resistance. It flicks to the side as an air rudder to help swerves and turns at speed.

Long tail provides balance at speed

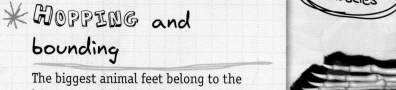

Powerful leg muscles

A kangaroo can cover more than 7 metres in one leap

✳ HOPPING and bounding

The biggest animal feet belong to the kangaroo, which bounds along at almost 60 kilometres per hour. Its pogo-stick style recycles energy stored in the legs' stretchy tendons (which link muscles to bones) and ligaments (which connect bones at a joint). As the kangaroo lands, these parts squash like pressed springs. Then they rebound and lengthen, giving out their stored energy to extend the legs and push the kangaroo up and forwards. This greatly reduces the effort needed for each bound.

Estimates of the cheetah's top speed are 96–101 km/h, compared to a champion human sprinter at 43 km/h.

To watch amazing footage of a cheetah hunting a Thomson's gazelle visit www.factsforprojects.com and click on the web link.

Second fastest to the cheetah is the pronghorn of North America. This antelope-like animal has a maximum speed of around 95 km/h but its stamina is greater than a cheetah's due to its big lungs and heart.

Head and ears Compared to other big cats, the cheetah has a relatively small head and ears in proportion to its long, rangy body. This provides extra streamlining.

The main leg muscle (blue) joins to the thigh bone farther from the hip joint

The main leg muscle (red) joins to the thigh bone very near the hip joint

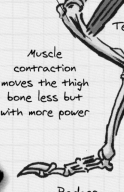

Teres major muscle

Muscle contraction moves the thigh bone less but with more power

Muscle contraction moves the thigh bone more but with less power

Badger

Cheetah

How do MUSCLES work BONES?

Most muscles are attached at each end to a bone, and the bones are linked by joints. When a muscle contracts it pulls its two bones closer together, working like two levers. The closer a muscle is attached to the joint, the more it moves the bone, which is called mechanical advantage. In the cheetah, a small but powerful contraction of the gluteus muscle in the hip pulls the upper leg bone, the femur, around in a large arc. This swings the leg backwards to push the paw against the ground and propel the cat forwards.

Strong wrist bones support the paws

Hips and shoulders The flexible hip and shoulder joints allow the upper leg bones to swing through half a circle – 180 degrees – for maximum length of stride.

Legs, paws and claws The legs and paws are long and slim, to swing to and fro with minimal effort. The claws are partly exposed for increased grip.

As well as being the fastest runner, the cheetah has incredible acceleration – from standstill to 100 km/h in three seconds – matching the best sports cars.

TAKING TO THE AIR

Like all animal movement, bird flight is powered by muscles – mainly the powerful pectorals in the chest. They pull down and twist the wings so their curved aerofoil shape gives both lift for staying up and thrust to move forwards. Some birds can fly for hours without flapping their wings. They aim into the wind and use air speed to soar up and move forwards.

Did you know?

Fastest of all animals is the peregrine falcon, with a power-dive or 'stoop' of 350 kilometres per hour. However the spine-tailed swift wins in level flight at 160 kilometres per hour, with a rather plump duck, the red-breasted merganser, a close second.

Shoulder The main wing joint is the shoulder, between the ends of the humerus or 'forearm' bone and the large coracoid bone that joins to the sternum.

The heaviest flying bird is the great bustard, at around 18 kg. The longest wings, with a span of 3.5 m, belong to the wandering albatross.

Wing bones The 'wrist' bones are flexible and allow the bird to twist and turn in flight. They are fused to the 'hand' bones, which are made up of three 'fingers' or digits. These digits are fused to provide strength in flight and support for feathers.

Furcula (wishbone)

Keel This flange on the breastbone or sternum provides a large surface area to anchor the main flight muscles into the body. It is made stronger by the V-shaped furcula or wishbone just in front of it.

Flight muscles

Beetles lift their wing cases to reveal two pairs of flight wings

✳ INSECT flight

Most insects have four wings rather than two, and they use a very different method of flapping. Each wing anchors into the middle section of the body, the thorax wall, at a swivel joint that has two click-stop positions – wing-up and wing-down. As two sets of muscles inside the thorax alternately pull, they bend the thorax wall in and out like a clickbox, which makes the wings flick up and down. Some tiny flies, such as midges, beat their wings more than 1000 times per second.

A bird's beak, feathers and claws are all made of the same substance as human hair and nails – keratin.

Watch an incredible clip of the Philippine eagle in flight by visiting www.factsforprojects.com and clicking on the web link.

Large birds flap their wings as slowly as once every second, making a whooshing sound. Small birds flap much faster, with hummingbirds reaching more than 80 beats per second, which generates the humming sound.

Primary feathers
The wingtip or primary feathers fan out to disrupt air flow, or fold together to smooth it, allowing the bird to make delicate adjustments as it glides.

Tail feathers Caudal or tail feathers fan out to work as an air brake, especially when the bird wants to slow down as it comes in to land.

Secondary feathers

Vane of feathers with central shaft

A typical large bird such as the bald eagle (above) has more than 7000 feathers. Some types of swan have over 20,000, but many are soft down feathers, under the main outer ones.

Wing's lift force is transmitted to main body

Smaller supracoracoideus muscle raises the wing

Humerus bone

Coracoid bone

Downstroke generates lift

Keel of breastbone

Big pectoralis muscle contracts to pull the wing down

How do FLIGHT MUSCLES work?

The two pairs of chief flight muscles in the chest run between the keel of the breastbone and the first bone in the wing, the humerus. The pectoralis muscle is below the humerus, and when it shortens, it lowers the bone, and so the whole wing, to force air down and generate lift. Then it relaxes and the supracoracoideus muscle just above it shortens. This action lifts the humerus by a tendon that loops over the top of the joint, for the upstroke. Less force is needed to raise the wing than to lower it on the power stroke, so the supracoracoideus muscle is smaller than the pectoralis.

MOVING IN WATER

Most fish thrust through the water with side-to-side swishes of the tail. Large V- and W-shaped blocks of muscles along the body, known as myotomes, contract on one side from head to tail, then the other side likewise, to make the central backbone arch left and right and wave the tail. In fast-swimming fish these muscles make up more than four-fifths of body weight.

Did you know?

As the speediest fish in the ocean, the sailfish – a close cousin of the marlin – is as fast as the cheetah on land. With its tall dorsal fin folded down along its body, it thrashes along at over 100 kilometres per hour. The seahorse is a real slowcoach at just 20 metres per hour.

Small reef fish specialize in darting around in all directions, with little need for straight-line speed. Their fins are usually large and easily fanned or folded for precise control.

Mouth and teeth Big predators such as the marlin chase mainly smaller fish such as sardines, pilchards and anchovies. They can swallow these whole and so have only small teeth.

Upper jaw

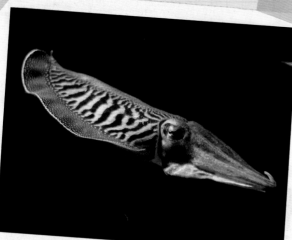

Cuttlefish squirt out a jet of water to surge backwards

✳ JET propelled

The mollusc group includes some of the fastest sea sprinters – squid, cuttlefish and octopus. They have a specialized method of movement. Water is sucked through a gap between the outer cloak-like mantle and the inner main body, into the mantle chamber. Then the mantle and body muscles squeeze the mantle chamber and squirt the water out of a narrow gap, the funnel, as a jet, propelling the animal backwards. Rapidly repeated, this makes the creature speed along in a series of jerks.

Streamlined bill The bill is a very long, sharply pointed upper snout or rostrum, and the lower jaw is also pointed. The marlin uses this 'spear' firstly to wound and stun its victims, which it then returns to eat.

Operculum (gill cover)

The striped marlin (above) can reach a massive 200 kg in weight and a length of 4 m. It is able to leap several metres above the sea's surface.

To watch slow-motion footage of the fastest fish in the world, the sailfish, visit www.factsforprojects.com and click on the web link.

Dorsal fin

✳ How do fish MOVE?

Fins are a fish's movement controllers. The dorsal or back fins, and the smaller anal fin on the underside near the tail, are all on the midline and prevent the fish rolling or leaning to the side. The other fins are paired: the pectorals on the sides near the head, and the pelvics behind them near the tail. These make the fish turn left or right, and rise or descend. The main forward thrust comes from the side surfaces of the body and the tail or caudal fin.

Dorsal fin stops the fish rolling

Tail helps to steer like the rudder on a boat

Pectoral fins can be used to steer and go up or down

Pushed water

Forward motion

Pushed water

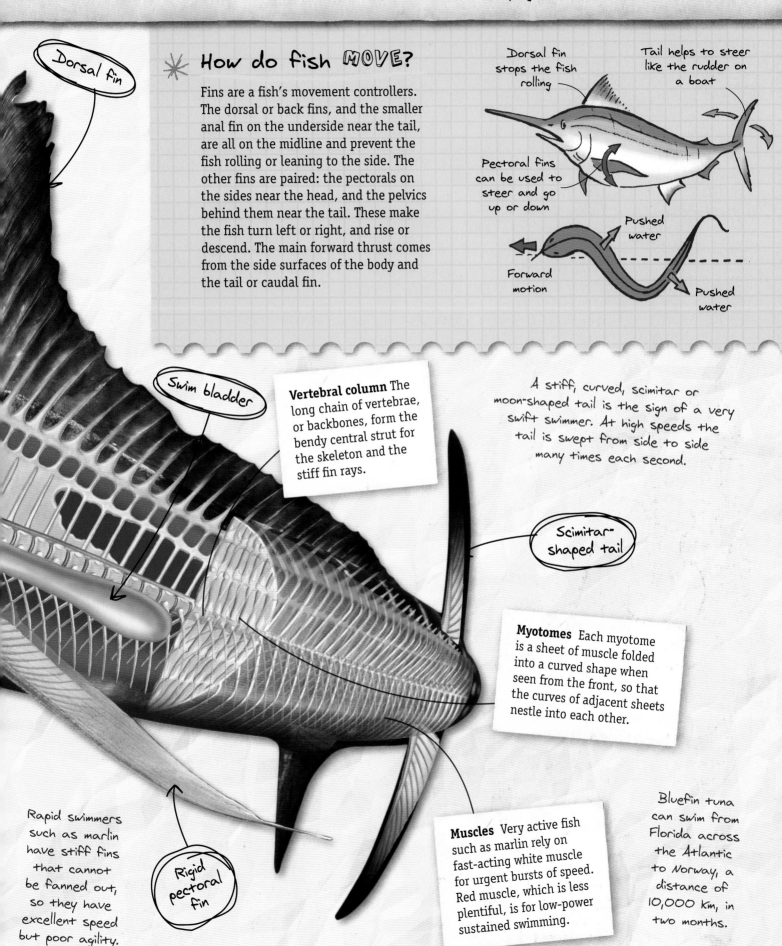

Swim bladder

Vertebral column The long chain of vertebrae, or backbones, form the bendy central strut for the skeleton and the stiff fin rays.

A stiff, curved, scimitar or moon-shaped tail is the sign of a very swift swimmer. At high speeds the tail is swept from side to side many times each second.

Scimitar-shaped tail

Myotomes Each myotome is a sheet of muscle folded into a curved shape when seen from the front, so that the curves of adjacent sheets nestle into each other.

Rapid swimmers such as marlin have stiff fins that cannot be fanned out, so they have excellent speed but poor agility.

Rigid pectoral fin

Muscles Very active fish such as marlin rely on fast-acting white muscle for urgent bursts of speed. Red muscle, which is less plentiful, is for low-power sustained swimming.

Bluefin tuna can swim from Florida across the Atlantic to Norway, a distance of 10,000 km, in two months.

BREATHING IN AIR

Apart from a few microbes, all life-forms – including plants – need oxygen to stay alive. They must have continuing supplies of this gas, which makes up one-fifth of air, since the body cannot store much in reserve. Most bigger land creatures have airways and lungs for taking in oxygen, called the respiratory system. In many creatures, air moving in and out of the lungs does another job too. It's used to produce sounds such as roars, growls, hisses, barks and howls.

Did you know?

Warm-blooded creatures, especially smaller ones, breathe much faster than cold-blooded animals. They need extra oxygen to 'slow-burn' food for body warmth. A shrew takes 300 breaths per minute, a hummingbird 400, but a cold-blooded gecko lizard just 30.

The loudest land animal is the howler monkey. Its piercing whoops carry up to 5 km across the upper layer, or canopy, of the South American rainforest.

Laryngeal sacs Gorillas, chimps and orang-utans have laryngeal pouches, which are hollow air chambers branching from the larynx into the neck and upper chest, to amplify vocal sounds.

The roar of a full-grown male gorilla or silverback (right), can be heard more than 2 km away even through dense forest.

At rest, a gorilla breathes in and out half a litre of air at a time. This increases to 5 litres when very active.

Ribs These play a vital role in protecting the lungs. Strip-like muscles between the ribs, known as intercostals, contract powerfully for deep breathing or when producing loud noises. In quiet breathing, the diaphragm does most of the work.

✳ How do INSECTS breathe?

An insect has a branching network of air tubes, called trachea, inside its body. These open to the outside at small holes known as spiracles along the sides of the body. There are no special breathing muscles. As the insect moves and changes body position, the air tubes squeeze and stretch to push stale air out and suck fresh air in. This unforced or passive method of breathing is one of the factors that limit how big insects can grow.

Caterpillars breathe through spiracles along their sides

Find out how the earliest animals evolved and developed lungs by visiting www.factsforprojects.com and clicking on the web link.

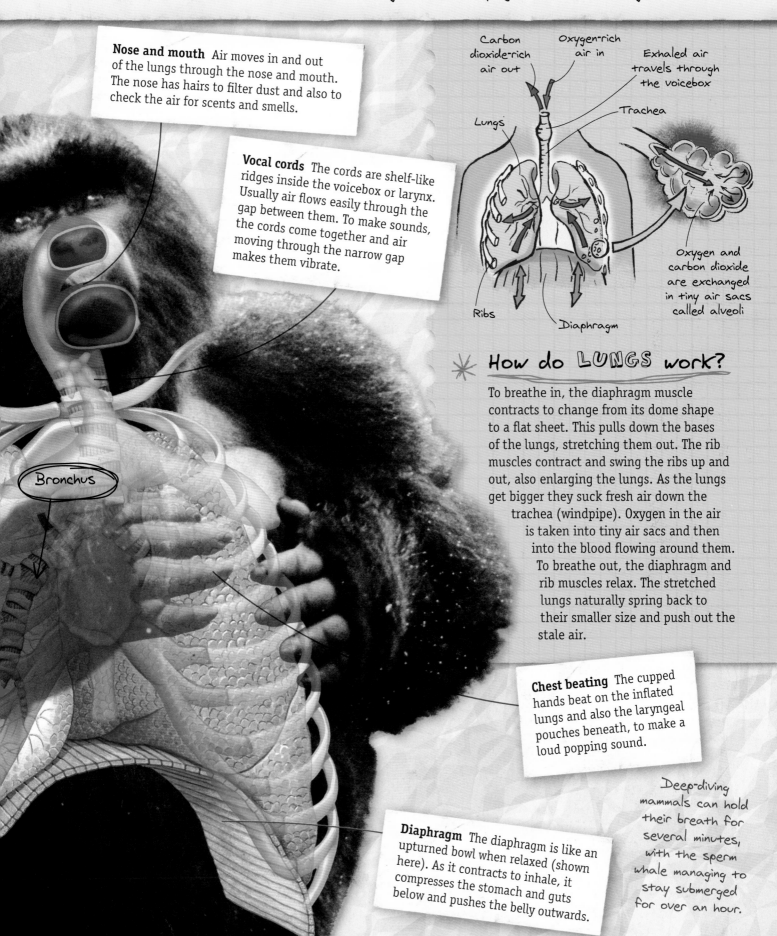

Nose and mouth Air moves in and out of the lungs through the nose and mouth. The nose has hairs to filter dust and also to check the air for scents and smells.

Vocal cords The cords are shelf-like ridges inside the voicebox or larynx. Usually air flows easily through the gap between them. To make sounds, the cords come together and air moving through the narrow gap makes them vibrate.

Carbon dioxide-rich air out

Oxygen-rich air in

Exhaled air travels through the voicebox

Lungs

Trachea

Oxygen and carbon dioxide are exchanged in tiny air sacs called alveoli

Ribs

Diaphragm

Bronchus

✳ How do LUNGS work?

To breathe in, the diaphragm muscle contracts to change from its dome shape to a flat sheet. This pulls down the bases of the lungs, stretching them out. The rib muscles contract and swing the ribs up and out, also enlarging the lungs. As the lungs get bigger they suck fresh air down the trachea (windpipe). Oxygen in the air is taken into tiny air sacs and then into the blood flowing around them. To breathe out, the diaphragm and rib muscles relax. The stretched lungs naturally spring back to their smaller size and push out the stale air.

Chest beating The cupped hands beat on the inflated lungs and also the laryngeal pouches beneath, to make a loud popping sound.

Deep-diving mammals can hold their breath for several minutes, with the sperm whale managing to stay submerged for over an hour.

Diaphragm The diaphragm is like an upturned bowl when relaxed (shown here). As it contracts to inhale, it compresses the stomach and guts below and pushes the belly outwards.

BREATHING IN WATER

Breathing takes oxygen into the body. There is plenty of oxygen in air – and in water too. Fish gills are frilly or feathery structures on the sides of the head, with a huge surface area for absorbing as much dissolved oxygen as possible. The gill surface is so thin, to allow oxygen to pass through easily, that it shows the oxygen-collecting blood flowing just beneath, making the gills appear red.

Did you know?

Some fish not only breathe with gills – they feed with them too. The gills have rows of comb-like rakers to filter food from the water. The world's biggest fish, the whale shark, is a gill-raking filter-feeder.

The breathing system of a fast, active shark, such as the blue shark, is up to ten times more efficient than that of a sluggish bottom-dwelling shark.

First dorsal fin

Second dorsal fin

✳ Un-hidden gills

Fish gills are hidden under flaps on the sides of the head. Crabs, octopus, shellfish, and many other aquatic animals have frilled or feather-like gills too. In crabs they are along the sides of the body under the main shell. Some animals with gills inside the body have regular muscle-powered pumping movements to replace low-oxygen 'used' water with new supplies high in oxygen. Other creatures, such as sea slugs and worms, have exposed gills that wave about and rely on water currents to bring new supplies of dissolved oxygen.

Heart

Stiff pectoral fin

Sea slugs have visible feathery gills

Gill filaments The tiny, delicate filaments or lamellae have extremely thin walls, so oxygen has less than one-fiftieth of one millimetre to travel from water to blood.

Gill bar arches The curved gill bars are, like the rest of the shark's skeleton, made of springy cartilage (gristle). Each supports a sheet-like gill septum, which is in turn held in place by another curved part, the gill bar.

To watch a video of a huge whale shark's gills in action
visit www.factsforprojects.com and click on the web link.

Most sharks have five pairs of gills but a few have six or seven — a primitive feature left over from their early evolution.

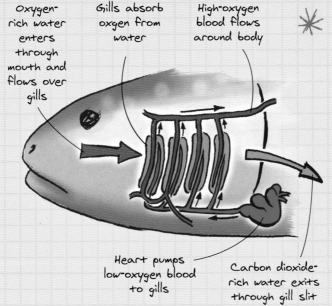

Oxygen-rich water enters through mouth and flows over gills

Gills absorb oxgen from water

High-oxygen blood flows around body

Heart pumps low-oxygen blood to gills

Carbon dioxide-rich water exits through gill slit

How do GILLS work?

Gills are similar to lungs, but instead of having millions of tiny air chambers, they have millions of leafy projections that water flows past. Because the concentration of oxygen is higher in the water than in the blood, oxygen passes into the blood within the projections, or lamellae. Waste carbon dioxide passes, or diffuses, the other way, into the water. The water then flows out through the gill slits, one per gill arch. In bony fish such as marlin, all the gills on one side are covered by a bony flap, the operculum, rather than having separate slits.

Lateral line detects movement in the water

Cartilaginous skull

Nostril A shark's nostrils do not lead through the nose into the throat, as in mammals. They are pit-like dead ends lined with smell sensors and play no part in breathing.

Pointed streamlined snout

Teeth are constantly replaced

The tiger shark (left) is a generally sluggish swimmer, but its muscles can burst into action for a sudden charge using 'spare' oxygen stored in its muscles and blood.

Electrosense Tiny hollows over the shark's snout sense faint natural electrical pulses sent out by the active muscles of nearby animals.

BRAIN AND NERVES

The more we learn about animals, the more we find out about how they learn. Measures of intelligent behaviour include step-by-step problem-solving and using tools. These depend on the brain to recognize a situation, work out what to do by trial and error, and remember it for next time, and also the nerves to control body muscles for deliberate and precise actions.

Did you know?

Humans once prided themselves on being the only creatures to use tools, but then chimps were seen using them. Birds such as the Egyptian vulture and woodpecker finch, dolphins, orang-utans, gorillas, elephants and capuchin monkeys have also been seen using tools.

The simplest animals are sponges, which have no brain or nerves. Jellyfish have a net-like system of nerves but no brain. Starfish have a simple ring-shaped brain.

Nerves to arm, hand and fingers

Even very small creatures such as fingernail-sized flatworms can be trained to get around a simple maze.

Spinal cord The main nerve from the brain is the spinal cord, which is inside the vertebrae (backbones). It sends nerve branches to all parts of the body.

✳ BRAIN TRAINING

Finding out how smart an animal is can involve putting it into an unnatural situation with a human-devised problem to solve, and providing a tasty treat as a reward. The octopus scores well here, able to recognize different shapes, colours and symbols on containers in order to win a meal. Another measure comes from watching creatures in nature and seeing how they tackle life's novel challenges. Again the octopus shows itself as a bright spark. For example, it uses a large empty shell as a protective shelter.

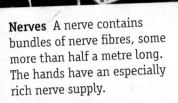

Nerves A nerve contains bundles of nerve fibres, some more than half a metre long. The hands have an especially rich nerve supply.

By carrying a shell as a shelter this octopus can protect itself

Discover more intelligent animals that use tools by visiting www.factsforprojects.com and clicking on the web link.

Upper brain The large, wrinkled upper part of the brain is the cerebrum. Its two halves are known as cerebral hemispheres. It deals with conscious thoughts, information coming in from the senses, and instructions going out to the muscles for movements.

Surface or cortex of cerebrum

Lower brain The ridged cerebellum at the base of the brain co-ordinates detailed control of muscles. Other lower centres of the brain deal with essential life processes such as breathing and heartbeat.

Tools Chimps use more than a dozen tools, such as rock hammers to crack open tough nuts on a flat stone, which acts as an anvil.

Animals with large brains compared to their bodies include dolphins, marmoset monkeys, shrews and some small birds, such as hummingbirds.

The chimpanzee's brain weighs 400 grams, which is about 1/120th of its body weight. In humans the brain is 1/45th of our body weight.

✳ Nerve MESSENGERS!

Nerves are like the body's wiring system, carrying messages in the form of tiny electrical pulses between the brain and all body parts. They are built up from single units called nerve cells or neurons. Each nerve cell has a main cell body, a nucleus or control centre, and short branching projections known as dendrites. These detect messages coming from other nerve cells. The messages are analyzed and sorted, then the resulting outgoing messages pass to a longer, thicker projection, the axon or nerve fibre, to reach other nerve cells.

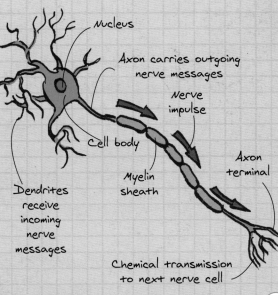

Nucleus

Axon carries outgoing nerve messages

Nerve impulse

Cell body

Axon terminal

Myelin sheath

Dendrites receive incoming nerve messages

Chemical transmission to next nerve cell

HEART AND BLOOD

Not all animals have a heart. Simple creatures such as jellyfish and sponges lack one. Then again, an octopus has three and an earthworm has five. But the worm's 'hearts' are really just muscular thickenings of blood vessel walls. A true heart has various chambers that suck in and pump out blood, and valves to make sure this blood always flows the correct way.

Did you know?

The biggest heart belongs to the biggest animal, the blue whale. It is the size of a compact family car, yet it is only 1/200th of the total body weight. It pumps about 10 tonnes of blood around the vast body. Tiny insects have hearts 50 times smaller than this full stop.

Dorsal fin

Veins These wide, floppy, thin-walled vessels carry blood back to the heart. The blood oozes along at low pressure, without the surges of high pressure found in arteries.

A dolphin's muscles contain a substance called myoglobin. Like haemoglobin in blood, this stores oxygen. It allows the muscles to keep working underwater, when the dolphin cannot breathe and its heartbeat is very slow.

Capillary network

Arteries Thick-walled and strong, arteries carry blood away from the heart. Their walls are also elastic, to absorb and even out the surges of pressure as blood is pumped out of the heart.

Vena cava (main vein)

The hummingbird's heart is 1/50th of its body weight

✳ A HEARTBEAT away

In warm-blooded creatures, heartbeat rate links to body size. A shrew's heart races along at 600 beats per minute, a hummingbird's at over 1000, while for a blue whale, it's ten or fewer. In turn, this links to the total number of beats in a lifetime. On average, bigger animals have slower heartbeat rates, but they live longer too. Most mammal hearts beat between one and two billion times in their lives. Humans score higher, partly because medical care keeps us going longer. Some of us exceed three billion beats in a lifetime.

Find out about different animal circulatory systems by visiting www.factsforprojects.com and clicking on the web link.

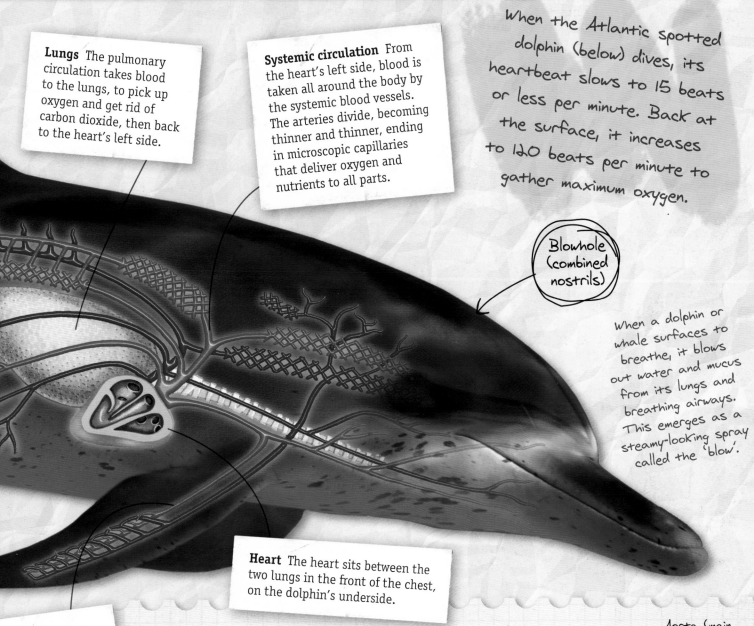

Lungs The pulmonary circulation takes blood to the lungs, to pick up oxygen and get rid of carbon dioxide, then back to the heart's left side.

Systemic circulation From the heart's left side, blood is taken all around the body by the systemic blood vessels. The arteries divide, becoming thinner and thinner, ending in microscopic capillaries that deliver oxygen and nutrients to all parts.

When the Atlantic spotted dolphin (below) dives, its heartbeat slows to 15 beats or less per minute. Back at the surface, it increases to 120 beats per minute to gather maximum oxygen.

Blowhole (combined nostrils)

When a dolphin or whale surfaces to breathe, it blows out water and mucus from its lungs and breathing airways. This emerges as a steamy-looking spray called the 'blow'.

Heart The heart sits between the two lungs in the front of the chest, on the dolphin's underside.

Blood The red colour is due to the substance haemoglobin. Combined with oxygen, blood is bright red; when low in oxygen it is a dull red-blue.

A dolphin has about twice the amount of haemoglobin in a drop of blood than a human does.

✳ How do HEARTS pump BLOOD?

Main veins known as vena cavae bring used, low-oxygen blood to the heart's right side. It flows into a small upper chamber, the right atrium, then through a one-way valve into the larger right ventricle. Meanwhile high-oxygen blood from the lungs arrives at the left side, where there are two similar chambers, the left atrium and ventricle, plus their valves. Strong muscles in the ventricle walls contract to squeeze blood out, from the right side to the lungs, and from the left side all around the body.

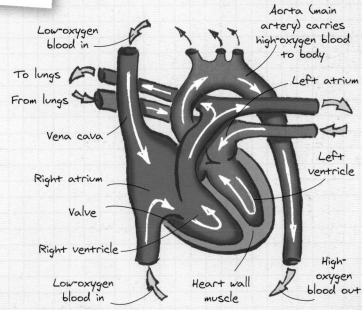

Low-oxygen blood in

Aorta (main artery) carries high-oxygen blood to body

To lungs

From lungs

Left atrium

Vena cava

Right atrium

Left ventricle

Valve

Right ventricle

Low-oxygen blood in

Heart wall muscle

High-oxygen blood out

W arm-blooded animals can stay active even in cold conditions, when cold-blooded creatures are hardly able to move. But this comes at a price. Body warmth is generated from energy in food, which means eating perhaps ten times more than a cold-blooded creature. In the coldest places, mammals need plenty of bodily adaptations to conserve heat.

Did you know?

Apart from birds and mammals, certain other creatures are 'warm-blooded' – at least, their bodies are warmer than their surroundings. They include certain moths that 'tremble' their wing muscles to make heat. Sharks such as the great white can be 10–15°C warmer than the ocean around them.

During an especially difficult winter, a polar bear can lose up to half its body weight, with males going from over 600 kg to nearer 300 kg.

The white fur of the polar bear provides excellent camouflage in the icy Arctic.

Underfur Under the outer guard coat is the thick, soft, dense underfur. The bear uses its teeth and paws to groom both outer and inner fur layers carefully, spread waterproofing oils and remove pests.

Blubber stores around hips

✳ Keeping COOL!

In the sunny, scorching tropics, mammals have the opposite problem to polar bears – they risk getting too hot. So instead of small extremities, like the polar bear, they have evolved large extremities such as feet, tails and ears. Elephants have the world's largest ears, with a rich blood supply to spread heat into the air. Flapping the ears helps elephants to stay cool. Jackrabbits, bat-eared and fennec foxes, jerboas and similar desert-dwellers use the same trick. An added benefit is that these outsized ears pick up the faintest sounds – either prey to eat or enemies to avoid.

A jackrabbit's oversized ears help to prevent overheating

Outer fur The outer layer of fur is called the guard coat. Its hairs are thicker, up to 15 cm long, quite stiff and give physical protection.

To watch polar bears living in their icy Arctic habitat visit www.factsforprojects.com and click on the web link.

On average, polar bear males weigh twice as much as females.

Blubber In a well-fed polar bear this fatty layer under the thick skin can be more than 10 cm thick. It is not only valuable insulation, but also works as an energy store for times when food is scarce.

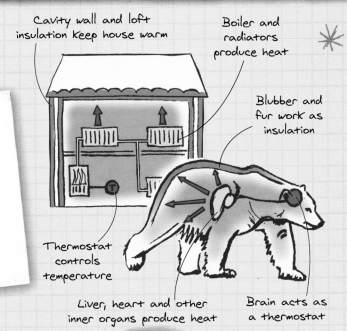

Cavity wall and loft insulation keep house warm

Boiler and radiators produce heat

Blubber and fur work as insulation

Thermostat controls temperature

Liver, heart and other inner organs produce heat

Brain acts as a thermostat

✳ Heat CONTROL

Some internal organs, notably the heart and liver, are always busy and so produce heat continually. It is the blood's task to spread this heat all around the body. Like a central heating thermostat, the brain monitors the temperature of the blood. If this starts to fall, the brain adjusts blood flow by sending nerve messages to certain arteries, which make the muscles in their walls contract. This narrows the artery and reduces blood flow to that part. Usually, less essential parts are shut down like this, such as the digestive system when it is not full of food. By controlling blood distribution, essential warmth is saved.

Head, ears and tail The bear's small, narrow head, and small ears and tail help to reduce heat loss in the cold air (or water) around it.

Under the thick fur coat, the polar bear's skin is black!

Polar bear fur looks white. But the hairs are in fact transparent with a hollow core, and scattered light makes them appear white. (In the same way, colourless snow crystals appear white.)

INSULATION

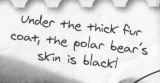

Erect hairs trap warm air next to body

Blood supply

Fat layer (blubber)

Hairy paws The soles of the massive paws – which can be 30 cm across in a big male – have a hairy covering on the thick skin. This helps to reduce heat loss to the ice and snow, and also increases grip on slippery ice.

THE POWER OF SIGHT

Apart from underground dwellers and deep-sea inhabitants, sight is a major sense for many creatures – from flies to moths, rats to cats, owls to humans. Evolution has come up with about six main designs of eyes for various animal groups. The structure of an insect's or squid's eye is very different from the eye design shown here, which is common to all vertebrates – fish, amphibians, reptiles, birds and mammals.

Did you know?

The largest eyes do not belong to the biggest animals, the great whales. Their eyes are only about the size of a large orange. The biggest eyes belong to the giant squid, which uses vision even in the ocean's gloomiest twilight zone where there is total darkness. The squid's eyeballs are 26–28 centimetres across, almost exactly the same as a soccer ball.

Owls can see in light levels ten times fainter than our own eyes detect.

Cornea The cornea and its thin covering, the conjunctiva, are delicate and sensitive. In birds, they are kept clean by a third eyelid called the nictitating membrane. This sweeps across the eye as the bird blinks.

DIAGRAM OF AN OWL'S EYE

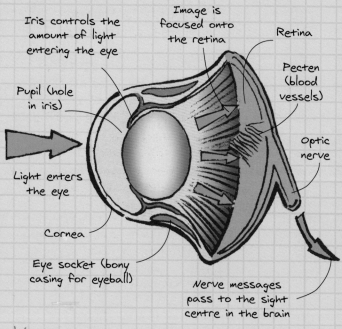

Iris controls the amount of light entering the eye

Image is focused onto the retina

Retina

Pecten (blood vessels)

Pupil (hole in iris)

Optic nerve

Light enters the eye

Cornea

Eye socket (bony casing for eyeball)

Nerve messages pass to the sight centre in the brain

How do EYES work?

In the typical vertebrate eye, light arrives through a clear domed 'window' at the front, the cornea. It passes through a thin fluid, a hole in the ring of muscle called the iris, and then through the rounded lens. This can change shape to focus the light rays clearly as they continue into the eyeball and shine onto its inner lining, the retina. The retina contains millions of light-sensitive cells that change the pattern of light rays into a similar pattern of nerve messages to send along the optic nerve to the brain.

'Horns' or 'ears' are just feather tufts

Short facial feathers

In an owl, the eyeballs take up more than half of the head, and so are bigger than the brain.

Read more facts about animals with incredible vision by visiting www.factsforprojects.com and clicking on the web link.

Iris Muscles in the coloured iris change size and so alter the pupil. They make the pupil smaller in bright light (as shown here) so too much light does not overpower and damage the retina inside.

Optic nerve The optic nerve is one of the shortest and thickest in the body, containing many millions of nerve fibres.

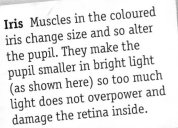

Retina

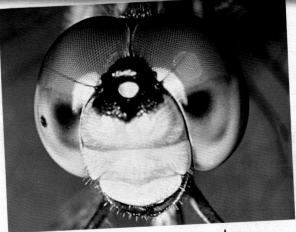

The dragonfly's compound eyes form half of its head

Pupil The pupil looks like a black spot, but in fact it is a circular hole in the middle of the iris, leading into the mostly dark interior of the eyeball.

Lens The lens, just behind the pupil, is pulled thinner by muscles around it to focus distant objects clearly onto the retina. It becomes thicker, almost spherical, to focus nearby objects.

✳ All-seeing EYES

The vertebrate eye is 'simple' in that it has just one lens and one light-sensitive layer, the retina. Insect eyes are 'compound' because they have many units, each with a form of lens and a light-sensitive layer. The individual rod- or cone-shaped units are called ommatidia and are arranged like pins in a pin cushion. One ommatidium detects only a small 'spot' of brightness and colour. But many of them together build small dots into a mosaic-like picture. A dragonfly has more than 30,000 ommatidia in each eye.

Owls' eyes are shaped more like tubes than balls. They cannot swivel easily in their sockets to look around. An owl has to move its whole head to see to the side — it can even turn its neck to look directly behind.

To look all around and up and down, the owl has a very bendy neck with 14 neck bones or vertebrae — twice as many as mammals.

ECHOLOCATION

The hours of darkness make it difficult for many animals to see – so this is when hearing comes into its own. For bats, ears are doubly important. These night-fliers listen not only for warning sounds of predators and other dangers, they also listen to navigate even in total darkness, by echolocation. So it is little wonder that bat hearing is amongst the most sensitive in the animal world.

Did you know?

Echolocation is not confined to bats. Ultrasonic clicks and squeaks are used by dolphins and some of their whale cousins to find prey and obstacles in murky water. Some shrews have developed a simple form of echolocation, as have birds such as cave swiftlets and oilbirds.

Outer ear The large ear flap is called the pinna. Bats use muscles around the base of the pinna to swivel it like a radar dish, sweeping to and fro to catch faint echoes from a wide area around.

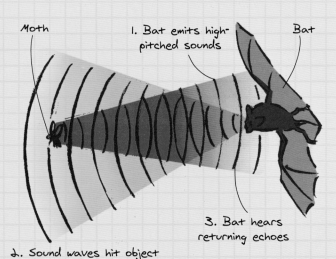

Moth

1. Bat emits high-pitched sounds

Bat

3. Bat hears returning echoes

2. Sound waves hit object and bounce or reflect back

Wing membrane (patagium)

Outgoing sounds The ultrasonic sounds are made in the voicebox (larynx). Most bats emit them from the mouth, but some use the nose too and 'aim' the sound beam with their nostrils.

Cockroach prey

✳ How does ECHOLOCATION work?

Ultrasounds are sounds that are too high-pitched or shrill for human ears. Bats emit ultrasonic clicks, squeaks and ticks that travel outwards. If any of these sound waves hit an object they reflect, or bounce off. The reflections or echoes pass through the air and some reach the bat's ears, which send nerve messages to its brain. Like a tiny high-speed computer, the brain analyzes the direction, strength and time delay of the echoes, and works out the size, distance and direction of the object. Locating objects by echoes in this way is called echolocation.

The pallid bat (right) not only has large ears to capture returning echoes, it also has large eyes compared to most bats.

To listen to echolocation sound patterns of different bats, whales and dolphins visit www.factsforprojects.com and click on the web link.

Thin, long arm bones are light but strong

Some long-eared bats have ears twice as large as their heads!

Brain

INNER EAR

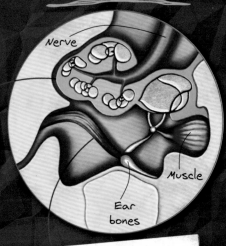

Nerve

Muscle

Ear bones

Cochlea Deep in the ear, the cochlea converts vibrations from the eardrum into nerve messages that flash along the auditory nerve to the brain.

Tragus This upright finger-like projection in the pinna helps to double-reflect and focus certain sound waves, especially those coming from above or below.

Eardrum The ear canal in the outer ear leads to the eardrum, a small, flexible sheet. This shakes or vibrates as sound waves bounce off it, and passes the vibrations to the inner parts of the ear.

Grasshoppers have 'ears' on their front knee joints

Bat squeaks 'sweep' from high to even higher pitch, or the other way around. The pitch, or frequency, of a returning echo tells the bat which part of the 'sweep' it comes from.

✳ WEIRD ears

Ears are not just flaps on the sides of a mammal's head. Birds have ears here too, under the feathers. Each ear is a patch of skin-like eardrum, the tympanum, without an ear flap around it. Reptiles and amphibians have similar patches. Fish have a stripe along each body side, the lateral line, that responds to sounds and other vibrations in water. Insects such as grasshoppers have tympani on their legs or sides of the abdomen (rear body), while scorpions have feathery ear-like sensors, called pectines, under the body.

SMELL AND TASTE

All around are tiny, floating particles in the air, such as pollen, fungus spores, dust – and smells. Smell particles, or odorants, are too small to see, but they carry information in the shapes of their chemical units, known as molecules. Animals' noses react to these odorants, and tongues similarly respond to flavorant particles in food.

Large, moveable ears

As well as smelling food, foxes sniff the urine and droppings of other foxes marking their territory, and also smell possible mates at breeding time.

Brain The brain has several 'smell centres' working together to process nerve messages from the nose. They include the amygdala in its lower centre and patches of the cortex covering the upper wrinkled cerebrum.

A fly can 'smell' with its feet

☀ SMELLY FEET!

A mammal's smell organs are handily placed at the entrance for air going down into the lungs. Creatures that do not have lungs may have their smell organs elsewhere, depending on their lifestyle. Flies and other insects have smell-detecting areas on their feet, which are usually the first parts to touch possible food. The fly detects at once if its landing site is tasty or not. The antennae of crabs and prawns also have smell sensors to pick up particles in the water.

Discover more animals with an amazing sense of smell by visiting www.factsforprojects.com and clicking on the web link.

Humans have about 10—12 million olfactory hair cells inside the nose. Dogs and foxes, with their long muzzles, have a much larger patch of olfactory epithelium with up to ten times more hair cells.

Olfactory epithelium
This patch in the lining of the nasal chamber contains millions of olfactory hair cells that respond to odorant particles floating in breathed-in air.

Olfactory bulb The olfactory bulb helps to sort smell information from the olfactory epithelium before it reaches the brain.

Nostrils take in air to smell

Tongue The tongue has thousands of microscopic clusters, called taste buds. Like smell, these have hair cells that respond to flavorants.

Nasal chamber
The chamber inside the nose is divided into two halves, left and right, by a middle wall of cartilage called the septum.

Fur can catch taste and smell particles

How does SMELL work?

During normal breathing, air flows smoothly in through the nostrils and the nasal chamber inside the nose, along to the windpipe and lungs. When an animal sniffs, air swirls around in the nasal chamber, bringing more smell particles into contact with the olfactory epithelium in its roof. The particles touch the micro-hairs of olfactory hair cells and, if the particle is of a particular kind of smell, stimulates the hair cell to produce a nerve message. Only certain smell particles stimulate certain hair cells. The brain analyzes the overall pattern to identify the smell.

Olfactory epithelium

Olfactory bulb

Brain

'Sniffed' air

Nasal chamber

Scent drawn in through nose

Air travelling to lungs

Tongue

Throat

SMELL TRANSFER

Olfactory bulb

Olfactory epithelium

Floating odorant particles

As a part-time scavenger, the red fox (left) has its nose tuned especially to old, rotting meat. In tough times it even sniffs and eats excrement.

TEETH AND JAWS

For all animals, getting food is at or near the top of the 'to-do' list. Only escaping danger, mating or protecting young might be higher. Mouthparts such as teeth, jaws and tongue are key. Plant eaters tend to have broad, flat-topped teeth for crushing their food. Meat eaters that pursue large prey need long, pointed front teeth to catch, hold and rip up their struggling victims, and shear-like rear teeth to slice sinew and chew gristle.

Did you know?

Most mammals, such as the hyaena, have just two sets of teeth – the milk or deciduous set and the adult or permanent set. But many reptiles and fish, such as crocodiles and sharks, continually grow hundreds of new teeth as old ones break, wear away or fall out.

Some fish lack jaws. Lampreys and hagfish have sucker-like mouths armed with small hooks to scrape and suck.

Crabs and other crustaceans have up to five sets of mouthparts to process their food.

The biggest teeth do not belong to a meat eater, but to the world's largest plant eater – they are the elephant's tusks.

The spotted hyaena (right) is famed as a scavenger, but in some areas more than half of its food is freshly hunted and killed by the hyaena itself.

Upper jaw The upper jaw, known as the maxilla, is joined to the bones of the skull above. The joint is not totally rigid; it has slight flexibility to absorb shocks and jarrs when cracking bone.

Lower jaw The mandible or lower jaw is the largest single bone in the head. It is also much more solid in internal construction and so heavier than other bones of similar size.

Teeth In big carnivores such as hyaenas, the rearmost upper premolar tooth, and the lower front molar tooth just beneath it, are extra-strong with tough ridges. They are called carnassial teeth and do most of the heavy-duty slicing.

Find out why different animals have different kinds of teeth by visiting www.factsforprojects.com and clicking on the web link.

Jaw muscles Two large muscles on each side close the jaws – the temporalis (indicated here) and the masseter (crossing over it). They are the most powerful muscles for their size.

The 'jaws' of insects, called mandibles, are much more varied than those of mammals, with many different shapes and designs. They work with a side-to-side action rather than up and down.

How do JAWS and TEETH work?

The upper and lower jaws pivot at the jaw joint to their rear. The muscles that close the jaws produce much more force at the rear, near the pivot, due to the lever effect. So the rear teeth, the premolars and molars, are specialized to shear and then crunch with huge power. At the front are the smaller incisors, for nibbling meat off bones or pests out of fur. Just behind are the long, pointed canines, which the predator uses to stab victims and cause gaping wounds.

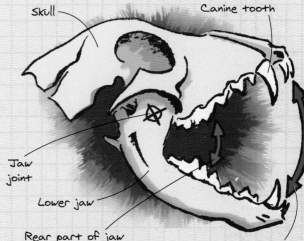

Skull

Canine tooth

Jaw joint

Lower jaw

Rear part of jaw exerts more force for molars to slice and crunch

Front part of jaw opens wide – ideal for grabbing

Jaw joint This works mainly in an up-down direction. However the lower jaw can move sideways to an extent, especially in herbivores such as horses.

Crocodiles have the most powerful bite in the animal world

MEAN MACHINES

Bite power is awkward to measure. It depends if the point pressure of individual teeth or all teeth is measured. It also depends if teeth at the front or the back of the mouth are measured, and also if this is done during a fast snap or a sustained crush. Overall, scientists estimate a powerful dog such as a rottweiler bites twice as hard as a human, a lion four times, a great white shark five, the hyaena six times, with the Nile crocodile at 15 times. *T rex* had an even stronger bite, 20 times, but luckily it's extinct!

USING VENOM

Venoms are harmful, even deadly substances that certain animals stab into their victims with teeth, claws, stingers or similar weapons. Snakes use their elongated teeth, called fangs, to do this. In rare cases of snakes biting humans, the snake does not strike for fun or to annoy us. It is defending itself against a much bigger – and, as far as the snake knows – possibly an even more dangerous creature about to kill and eat it.

Did you know?

There are several different kinds of venoms or toxins. Haemotoxins clot or disrupt blood flow. Neurotoxins affect nerves and muscles, paralyzing breathing and heartbeat. Proteolytic toxins dissolve tissue, such as muscles and other body parts.

When ready to attack prey, or preparing to defend, vipers assess each biting situation. They work out whether they should bite hard and long, or just give a quick stab, and if it should be a 'dry strike' without venom, or a real injection of venom.

Main upper jaw (pterygoid) bone

Maxilla This is the bone that tilts the fang to strike. Through it comes venom from the venom glands, which are a specialized form of salivary gland – venom is a deadly type of spit.

Fangs These are extra-long teeth. They are only exposed for a split second during the strike, then they are folded away safely again.

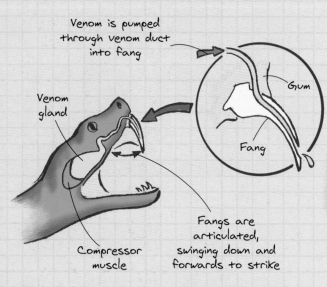

Venom is pumped through venom duct into fang

Venom gland

Gum

Fang

Compressor muscle

Fangs are articulated, swinging down and forwards to strike

✳ Articulated FANGS

Vipers have the most complicated venom system of any snakes. The two fangs normally lie flat, one on either side of the roof of the mouth, protected by a fleshy sheath. As the viper strikes, muscles at the base of each fang tilt the small bone at the fang's base. This makes the bone and fang arc down and forwards so the fang sticks out at the front of the mouth. As the fang jabs into the victim, compressor muscles around the venom gland tense to squeeze the gland. This forces venom along the venom duct, down through the hollow fang and into the victim.

The biggest venomous snake, more than 5 m long, is the king cobra. Its main prey is snakes, including other cobras.

Prey is soon paralyzed

Watch a video of an eyelash viper striking by visiting www.factsforprojects.com and clicking on the web link.

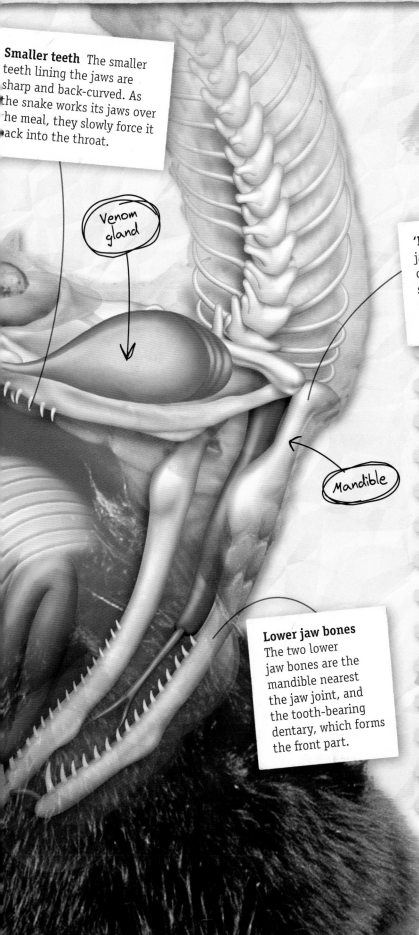

Smaller teeth The smaller teeth lining the jaws are sharp and back-curved. As the snake works its jaws over the meal, they slowly force it back into the throat.

Venom gland

The eyelash viper (left) increases its hunting success by keeping very still — except for flicking its tail to attract curious small creatures such as mice and birds.

'Dislocating' jaw joints The jaw joints do not so much come apart as tilt outwards on strut-like bones, the quadrates, allowing a huge gape for striking and swallowing.

Cobras also have front fangs, like vipers, but these are fixed in place and cannot tilt.

Mandible

✳ Who's most VENOMOUS?

Which is the most venomous animal? It depends. Some animals have powerful venom but not an especially strong bite or sting. Others have weak venom, but lots of it, which they deliver with great force. Usually near the top of the 'most venomous' list is the stonefish, which lurks in tropical shallows like a seaweedy rock. Other deadly contenders are the 2-metre-long inland taipan snake of Australia, the hand-sized Brazilian wandering spider, the pale yellow deathstalker scorpion of North Africa and the Middle East and the almost transparent box jellyfish.

Lower jaw bones The two lower jaw bones are the mandible nearest the jaw joint, and the tooth-bearing dentary, which forms the front part.

The blue-ringed octopus has enough venom to kill 20 people

DIGESTING FOOD

Apart from small, thin-skinned water creatures, which absorb food from their surroundings, most animals have guts. The basic gut design is a long tube from the mouth at the 'in' end to the anus at the 'out' end. It usually has specialized regions such as a crop, gullet or stomach to store big meals, and an intestine where food is broken down into tiny particles small enough to be absorbed by the body.

Did you know?

Simple creatures such as anemones have one digestive opening. This serves as both the mouth when they eat and the anus when they excrete. However the digestive tube of a manatee (sea cow) is 40 metres long.

Frogs' eyes bulge from their head partly for better vision and partly to keep them out of harm's way as prey struggles, kicks and squirms just beneath them.

Bulging eye

Dragonfly prey

A starfish feeds on the soft innards of a shellfish

✳ Inside OUT!

Not all animals digest their food inside their bodies. Many flies squirt digestive spit onto their meal, then mop up the soup-like result with their sponge-like mouthparts. Spiders stab venom and digestive juices into their prey, which dissolve the flesh for sucking up. The starfish goes one better. It prises open the protective shell of a mussel, clam or similar victim. Then it turns its stomach inside out through its mouth onto the meal, and slowly dissolves and absorbs the soft parts over several hours.

Mouth With only tiny teeth in its upper jaw to help grip its meal, the frog relies on strong bite power, its tongue and plenty of slime.

Oesophagus When prey is subdued, the frog gulps it down to its oesophagus, or gullet. This is helped by the frog retracting its eyeballs.

A common frog can eat more than 100 small flies in one day, which is enough to keep it going for up to one week.

Learn about the digestive systems of different animals including snakes, molluscs and insects by visiting www.factsforprojects.com and clicking on the web link.

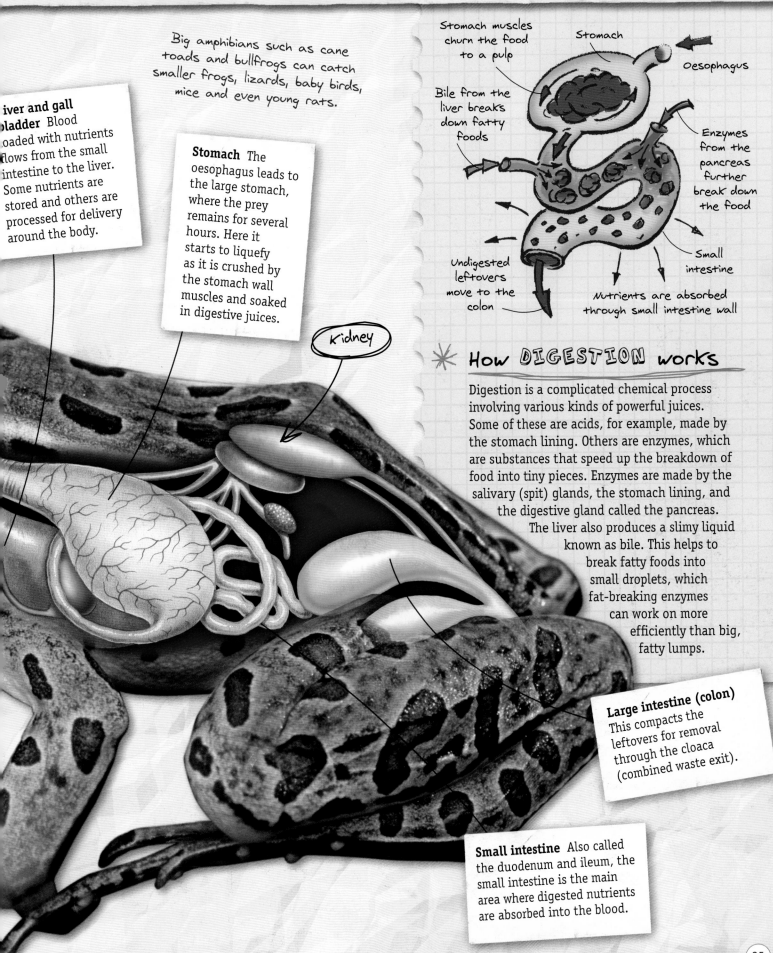

Big amphibians such as cane toads and bullfrogs can catch smaller frogs, lizards, baby birds, mice and even young rats.

iver and gall bladder Blood oaded with nutrients flows from the small intestine to the liver. Some nutrients are stored and others are processed for delivery around the body.

Stomach The oesophagus leads to the large stomach, where the prey remains for several hours. Here it starts to liquefy as it is crushed by the stomach wall muscles and soaked in digestive juices.

Kidney

Stomach muscles churn the food to a pulp

Stomach

Oesophagus

Bile from the liver breaks down fatty foods

Enzymes from the pancreas further break down the food

Small intestine

Undigested leftovers move to the colon

Nutrients are absorbed through small intestine wall

✳ How DIGESTION works

Digestion is a complicated chemical process involving various kinds of powerful juices. Some of these are acids, for example, made by the stomach lining. Others are enzymes, which are substances that speed up the breakdown of food into tiny pieces. Enzymes are made by the salivary (spit) glands, the stomach lining, and the digestive gland called the pancreas. The liver also produces a slimy liquid known as bile. This helps to break fatty foods into small droplets, which fat-breaking enzymes can work on more efficiently than big, fatty lumps.

Large intestine (colon) This compacts the leftovers for removal through the cloaca (combined waste exit).

Small intestine Also called the duodenum and ileum, the small intestine is the main area where digested nutrients are absorbed into the blood.

REPRODUCTION

Giving birth is not that common in the animal world. Most mammals do, as do some insects, certain fish, reptiles and even worms. But the majority of animals reproduce by laying eggs. The egg is a survival capsule for the developing young, or embryo, inside. Nearly all birds take great care of their eggs, and also of the chicks when they hatch.

Did you know?

The biggest bird egg belongs to the ostrich and is 17 centimetres long – each one is the volume of 25 hen's eggs. The tiniest egg is the bee hummingbird's, and is one centimetre long. The largest egg compared to the size of the female belongs to the kiwi, at one-quarter of her body weight.

Usually the female bird builds the nest, incubates the eggs to keep them warm, and feeds the chicks. But the male rhea does all these duties without female help.

Sperm fertilizing egg

Birds such as kiwis and some eagles lay only one egg each year and provide great care for the chick. The slowest breeding bird is the albatross, which produces just one egg every two years.

Magnum The longest part of the reproductive system, this coiled tube has many tiny glands in its lining that produce albumen and minerals such as calcium to cover the egg.

Albumen (white) and yolk

Gamebirds such as the sand grouse (right) and partridges lay more than 20 eggs in each set, or clutch, and sometimes two or three clutches each year.

Shell gland During the whole egg production process, which takes 24–30 hours, the egg stays here for longest, usually 20–24 hours. The gland produces the hard, chalky shell around the egg, which hardens and finally becomes more brittle after laying.

Cloaca Birds have just one opening, the cloaca, for male sperm coming in, eggs going out, and also digestive and urinary wastes. The white, pasty 'poo' of birds is in fact a form of urine.

See incredible images of animals developing inside the womb or egg
by visiting www.factsforprojects.com and clicking on the web link.

The biggest-ever eggs were probably those of dinosaurs, some of which were over 30 cm long.

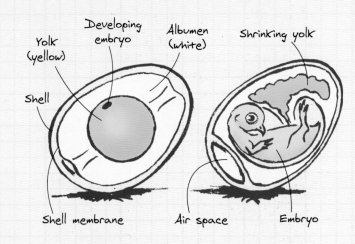

Yolk (yellow)

Developing embryo

Albumen (white)

Shrinking yolk

Shell

Shell membrane

Air space

Embryo

Oviduct This is the general name for the long tube or tract leading from the ovary. Its first section is the funnel-shaped infundibulum which takes the egg from the ovary.

Ovary This is the egg-producing part of the reproductive system. In most birds one of the ovaries, generally the right one, remains small and inactive. However it can become active if the left ovary is damaged.

How do EMBRYOS develop?

Animals breed when an egg cell from the female joins with a sperm cell from the male, known as fertilization. The fertilized egg starts to develop into an early stage of the offspring, known as the embryo. Its cells divide and grow, making it bigger. They move around, become specialized into different types such as blood cells, muscle cells and nerve cells, and start to shape the body parts. In many animals, including birds, the mother's reproductive system produces a store of nutrients and energy, called yolk, as food for the embryo. In mammals, food comes from the mother's blood through the placenta (afterbirth).

Soft breast feathers for egg incubation

MOTHERING father

We are familiar with animals caring for their babies because it happens in all mammals, and most birds too. But for other animal groups such as snakes, most fish, spiders and snails, parental care is incredibly rare. Where it does happen, usually it's the task of the mother alone. So one of the most unusual parents is the seahorse. The female releases her eggs into a pocket-like flap called the brood pouch on the front of her male partner. Here the eggs develop and hatch into tiny babies. The father then 'gives birth' by shaking himself violently as the babies shoot out of the pouch.

A seahorse father gives birth to hundreds of youngsters

GLOSSARY

Artery
A blood vessel that carries blood away from the heart and around the body.

Axon
The long, thin part of a nerve cell or neuron carries away nerve signals to pass them on to other nerve cells.

Blubber
A layer of fat under the skin of certain animals, mainly mammals and birds, which works as insulation to keep in body warmth and keep out excessive cold.

Canines
Long, sharp teeth near the front of the mouth, used for jabbing and stabbing.

Carnassial teeth
Specialized premolar and molar teeth near the rear of the mouth in meat-eating mammals such as the cat and dog families. The teeth are shaped to slice and shear with huge power.

Cerebellum
The lower rear part of the brain in many animals, especially birds and mammals, which co-ordinates the nerve signals going out to muscles to make complicated actions.

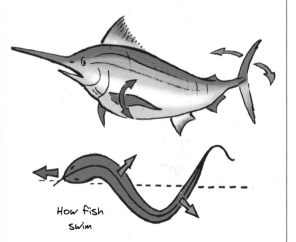

How fish swim

Cerebrum
The upper part of the brain in many animals, especially birds and mammals, which analyzes information from the senses and decides which actions to take.

Cloaca
The body opening in animals such as birds, reptiles and amphibians, through which waste such as urine and faeces pass out, and reproductive cells such as sperm and eggs pass through.

Cochlea
The coiled part deep in the ear that changes the patterns of sound waves vibrating it into nerve signals to send to the brain.

Cornea
The domed, clear front of the eye through which light rays pass and are part-focused before going through the lens for fine focusing.

Fangs
Long, sharp teeth used as feeding weapons possessed by various animals from snakes to spiders, often used to inject venom.

Fertilization
The moment when an egg cell from a female animal joins with a sperm cell from a male of the same species, and starts growing into a baby.

Gills
Body parts specialized to take in oxygen from water, in creatures such as fish, water worms and shellfish. They are usually delicate, frilly and branching.

Gluteus
The main muscle in the hip and upper leg that provides the power for movement, such as walking and running.

Incisors
Teeth at the front of the mouth, usually sharp and straight-edged, used for nibbling and gnawing.

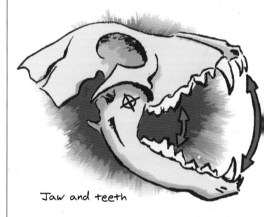

Jaw and teeth

Large intestine
Part of the gut, usually short and wide, which absorbs water, vitamins and minerals from digested food, and converts the remains into waste, ready for removal as faeces.

Lungs
Body parts specialized to take in oxygen from air and pass it to the blood. In mammals and birds, the lungs are in the chest, but in spiders they are on the underside of the body.

Mandible
The lower jaw or lower set of mouthparts in many animals, from mammals to insects.

Maxilla
The upper jaw or upper set of mouthparts in many animals, from mammals to insects.

Myotomes

Blocks of folded muscles along the bodies of animals such as fish and snakes.

Oesophagus

Also called the gullet, the first part of the guts after the mouth and throat in many animals, leading down to the stomach.

Olfactory epithelium

The smell-sensitive layer inside the nose, which changes the information from received smell particles into patterns of nerve signals to send to the brain.

Pectoralis

The main muscles in the chest area that flap a bird's wings down or make a mammal's front limbs reach and pull.

Pharynx

Part of the breathing and digestive systems in many animals, after the mouth and before the oesophagus. In mammals it is usually called the throat.

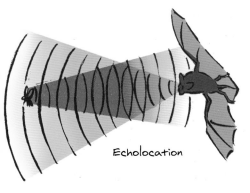

Echolocation

Pupil

The hole in the ring of muscle called the iris in the eye, through which light passes to the lens and inside of the eyeball.

Retina

The light-sensitive layer inside the eyeball that changes the patterns of light rays falling on it into patterns of nerve signals to send to the brain.

Segments

The sections along the bodies of animals such as caterpillars and worms, where each one has much the same structure as those in front and behind.

Skeleton

The strong supporting framework of an animal. In mammals, birds and most fish it is inside the body and made of bone. In creatures such as insects and crabs, it forms a hard outer casing.

Small intestine

Part of the gut, usually long, thin and coiled, which absorbs nutrients from digested food into the blood.

Spiracle

A breathing hole found in various animals such as some fish and insects, where air or water enters the body so that oxygen can be absorbed.

Swim bladder

A spongy, gas-filled organ in the body of most fish, where gas bubbles can be adjusted to make the fish lighter or heavier for the correct buoyancy.

Taste buds

Microscopic bundles of cells normally found on the tongue that detect flavour particles. In some animals, such as fish, taste buds are on the inside of the mouth – and even on the outside of the head and body.

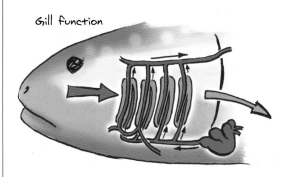

Gill function

Thorax

The middle section of an animal's body, such as the chest of a mammal. An insect's wings and legs are attached to its thorax.

Ultrasonic

Sound waves that are too high-pitched, or too short in wavelength, for the human ear to detect.

Vein

A blood vessel that carries blood towards the heart.

Venom

A chemical substance made by an animal that is bitten, stung or jabbed into another creature, to cause harm such as paralysis or even death.

Vertebrae

Backbones, the long chain of linked bones that make up the spinal column in mammals, birds, reptiles, amphibians and fish.

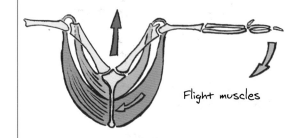

Flight muscles

INDEX